ADVANCED ENGLISH

Workbook

Level 8

SCHOLASTIC
New York Toronto London Auckland
Sydney New Delhi Hong Kong

Published by Scholastic India Pvt. Ltd.
A subsidiary of Scholastic Inc. New York, 10012 (USA).
Publishers since 1920, with international operations in Canada, Australia, New Zealand, the United Kingdom, India, and Hong Kong.

For information regarding permission, write to:
Scholastic India Pvt. Ltd.
A-27, Ground Floor, Bharti Sigma Centre,
Infocity-I, Sector-34, Gurgaon 122001 (India)

Series editor: Aishwarya Subramanian
Layout, design and typesetting by Ram Das Lal

First edition: October 2010
Reprint: January 2011; September 2011; March 2012; January ; November 2015 ; November 2017 ; October 2019 2023
ISBN-13: 978-81-8477-634-8

Printed at Shivam Offset Press, New Delhi

Contents

Introduction

The *Advanced English* workbooks are aimed at students of classes six, seven and eight. These books are intended to be used alongside the *Advanced English* course books. They focus on developing the student's basic comprehension, vocabulary, grammar and writing skills.

Each workbook is divided into seven sections based on the themes provided in the *Advanced English* course book. Each of these sections contains extensive practice exercises reflecting the topics covered in the course book.

Comprehension: Each section features one or more texts that are related to the theme of the section. Each of these texts is accompanied by a number of comprehension questions, with space for writing the answers provided within the book itself.

Vocabulary: There are innovative vocabulary exercises related to the themes provided. These include using the dictionary, solving word grids and crossword puzzles, and increasing familiarity with idiomatic English.

Grammar: The grammar sections contain useful practice exercises for the grammar topics covered in the main syllabus. The basic principles are restated at the beginning of the exercise in order to aid in revision, and space is provided in the book for writing answers. Answers to the comprehension, vocabulary and grammar sections are provided in the Teacher's Manual.

Writing: The writing sections aim to familiarise students with a wide range of writing formats, including formal and informal letters, diary entries, summaries and reviews. Sample texts are given and ample writing space is provided. In addition, there are creative writing exercises that allow the student to give rein to the imagination and to express himself or herself.

Art and literature have always shared a symbiotic relationship. Such a cross-pollination of genres not only enriches the former, but informs the latter. Many visual learners will find that these connections allow for better retention of the material and enable an engagement that is above mere rote-learning. It is for this reason that we chose to use cover images based on some of the world's great artwork. The cover of this book is based on the painting "Hamsa Damayanthi" by Raja Ravi Varma. Raja Ravi Varma was born in 1848 in the former princely state of Travancore. He is best known for his paintings of Indian mythological scenes.

1 Friendship

Comprehension

Read the poem and answer the questions.

Stately, kindly, lordly friend,
        Condescend
Here to sit by me, and turn
Glorious eyes that smile and burn,
Golden eyes, love's lustrous meed,
On the golden page I read.

All your wondrous wealth of hair,
        Dark and fair,

Silken-shaggy, soft and bright
As the clouds and beams of night,
Pays my reverent hand's caress
Back with friendlier gentleness.

Dogs may fawn on all and some
    As they come;
You, a friend of loftier mind,
Answer friends alone in kind.
Just your foot upon my hand
Softly bids it understand.

Morning round this silent sweet
    Garden seat
Sheds its wealth of gathering light,
Thrills the gradual clouds with might,
Changes woodland, orchard, heath,
Lawn, and garden there beneath.

Fair and dim they gleamed below:
    Now they glow
Deep as even your sunbright eyes,
Fair as even the wakening skies.
Can it not or can it be
Now that you give thanks to see?

May not you rejoice as I,
    Seeing the sky
Change to heaven revealed, and bid
Earth reveal the heaven it hid
All night long from stars and moon,
Now the sun sets all in tune?

What within you wakes with day
    Who can say?
All too little may we tell,
Friends who like each other well,
What might haply, if we might,
Bid us read our lives aright.

—*"To a Cat" by Algernon Charles Swinburne*

1 Answer the following questions.

i Who is the "friend" referred to by the poet?

____

____

ii Why does the poet describe the cat as a "friend of loftier mind"? How does he prove this?

____

____

iii What do you think the cat's foot on the poet's hand "softly bids it understand"?

____

____

iv What adjectives does the poet use to describe the cat?

____

____

v Why are the cat and the poet able to tell each other "all too little"?

____

____

Read the poem and answer the questions.

When a friend calls to me from the road
And slows his horse to a meaning walk,
I don't stand still and look around
On all the hills I haven't hoed,
And shout from where I am, What is it?
No, not as there is a time to talk.
I thrust my hoe in the mellow ground,
Blade-end up and five feet tall,
And plod: I go up to the stone wall
For a friendly visit.

—*"A Time to Talk" by Robert Frost*

2 Answer the following questions.

i What do you think the poet means by "a meaning walk"? Why does the friend slow his horse?

____

ii What do you think is the speaker's occupation?

iii How does the speaker react when a friend calls him?

iv Why do you think the poem is titled "A Time to Talk"?

Vocabulary

1 Find synonyms for the following words in the poems.

i stoop

ii higher

iii ripe

iv worshipful

v grassland ______________________

vi amazing ______________________

vii walk ______________________

viii payment ______________________

2 Use each of the words above in a sentence of your own.

____

____

____

____

____

____

____

____

____

____

____

Grammar

Conjunctions

Conjunctions are words that are used to join two or more conjunctions within the same sentence. There are various types of conjunctions:
Coordinating conjunctions join parts of a sentence that are grammatically equal.
Correlative conjunctions are made of two or more words which usually surround an adjective or verb.
Subordinating conjunctions join two clauses where one is dependent on the other.

1 Join the following sentences with the help of the conjunctions provided in the brackets:

i Aishwarya did not enjoy the camel ride. Hannah did not enjoy the camel ride. (neither ... nor)

____

ii Raghav was upset. He had left his bag at the guest house. (because)

____

iii They had to give up the camping expedition. There was a thunderstorm. (so)

____

iv Anjali packed the suitcases. Manav packed the suitcases. Shikha had a bath. (and, while)

____

v She is coming here next month. She should bring warm clothes. (if)

____

vi Bhuvan was tired. He fell asleep on the way home. (so ... that)

____

vii There are many tourists. Jaisalmer is a beautiful city. (although)

____

viii You cannot leave. We have had dinner. (until)

____

Writing

1 All the punctuation has been removed from the passage below. Rewrite the passage punctuating it so that it makes sense.

the russian gentleman was better the next day and the day after that better still and on the third day he was well enough to come into the garden a basket chair was put for him and he sat there dressed in clothes of fathers which were too big for him but when mother had hemmed up the ends of the sleeves and the trousers the clothes did well enough his was a kind face now that it was no longer tired and frightened and he smiled at the children whenever he saw them they wished very much that he could speak english mother wrote several letters to people she thought might know whereabouts in england a russian gentlemans wife and family might possibly be not to the people she used to know before she came to live at three chimneys she never wrote to any of them but strange people members of parliament and editors of papers and secretaries of societies and she did not do much of her story writing only corrected proofs as she sat in the sun near the russian and talked to him every now and then the children wanted very much to show how kindly they felt to this man who had been sent to prison and to siberia just for writing a beautiful book about poor people they could smile at him of course they could and they did but if you smile too constantly the smile is apt to get fixed like the smile of the hyena and then it no longer looks friendly but simply silly so they tried other ways, and brought him flowers till the place where he sat was surrounded by little fading bunches of clover and roses and canterbury bells

2 Communication

Comprehension

Read the extract and answer the questions.

I decided to run away. I took a bus to Lodhi Gardens. My plan was to sit in the park and feel sorry for myself. It worked. I felt very sorry for myself in no time.

"Heavy, isn't it?" I heard someone say. I looked up and there was a kindly old man, very thin, with an even thinner walking stick. "The world," he went on, "the weight of which you seem to be carrying on your young shoulders."

Wary of strangers, I nodded.

"What's wrong?" He asked.

"It's a curse," I said, *"I am speaking only in verse."* I didn't expect him to understand but I felt too tired to explain everything in detail. Besides, it would sound funny in verse.

Amazingly, he seemed to understand instantly.

"It's that age," he said. "In my time, this was very common, but now with modern medicine, people have forgotten about these problems."

I had no idea what he was talking about.

"You have an alternative disease," he said.

"An alternative disease," said I, *"spare me please."*

He was patient; he said, "I know it sounds strange; you have heard of alternative medicine—ayurveda, homeopathy? Anyway," he went on, "you have an alternative disease that modern medicine does not recognise. The only person remaining in Delhi who can help you is in Karol Bagh. I can take you there if you like."

I didn't like this at all. Talking to strangers was fine but going with them to Karol Bagh seemed somewhat excessive. But nobody else seemed to be taking this seriously.

He took me to an old office with no one inside except a man with an enormous head wearing ginormous glasses.

"I am Dr Ganpatadhikary," he said gravely. "What can I do you for you today?" He had an oddly comforting air about him and I told my whole sorry tale.

"Alternative diseases," he began, "are caused by bacteria which have a strain of playfulness in them. They have to be *fooled*, not treated".

This man is a crank, I said to myself, feeling very foolish for coming here.

The doctor was caught up in his own diagnosis.

"Your condition is something called Allergic Rhymitis," he said, "and is a tricky one to handle."

"Allergic Rhymitis?" I cried. *"What kind of joke is this?"*

Dr Ganpatadhikary said, "My son, it's not a joke. We will have to find a way of fooling this disease."

"How can we fool a disease? Can you explain it to me please?"

"Take the example of another alternative disease," the doctor said. "Infective Burstitis; a condition in which the patient cannot touch a balloon without bursting it. It can make you a social outcast at birthday parties. And Holi," he said as an afterthought. "We make the patient wear gloves with little needles on them. So when the balloons burst, it is because of the needles and not the disease. This infuriates the disease and it walks off in a sulk. We have to find a similar answer for you."

"Let's try this," he said. "Instead of trying to speak normally, try to deliberately speak in rhyme. Let's see if we can make it boring for the bacteria. Say something about the weather, in verse."

"Yesterday it rained pretty hard, it was all wet and slushy in my yard," was my instant reply. I didn't even have to try.

Dr Ganpatadhikary was not pleased and he went silent for a longish while.

"This is trickier than I thought," he said. "Okay, let's try and change the pattern of the rhyme. Instead of the a-a-b-b pattern, you know—where every line rhymes with the next—why don't you try to make every alternate line rhyme? Maybe we can gradually wean the bacteria away one line at a time? Try the a-b-a-b pattern. Let's try something about doctors," he said with a hint of mischief on his massive face.

That didn't work either. I found myself rhyming the second line all the time. For instance, I would go:

"The doctor's methods make me wonder as to which anaesthesia I am under, won't it make me flounder, if the doctor makes a blunder?"

or

"I passionately hate all injections they send me off into dejection, do you think it is purely projection, or a reasonable rejection?"

Not great poetry, I grant you, but the urge to rhyme every line just didn't go.

The doctor looked worried and whispered something to the old uncle who also looked worried. They went into a conference for five minutes.

Finally, the doctor looked at me and said, "We are going to try one last thing. It is a stupid idea." (Right, as if the others weren't.) "But it's the only hope we have left. We want you to rhyme the first part of your sentences and not the last. If we reverse the rhyme, maybe we will find the antidote to your disease."

"Try anything at least once," I began, meaning to start the next sentence with "cry" to rhyme with "try". But what came out was, *"Even if you feel like a dunce."*

There I was, rhyming again. The two kind old men looked crestfallen. I was doomed to rhyme till eternity. I got up and was preparing to leave when a thought struck me. It was an absolutely truly idiotic idea but it was an idea. If the whole trick was to reverse things, what if I looked at a mirror while trying this out?

"Is there a mirror anywhere close by? I have to make this one final try," I asked the doctor.

He took me to a small, ornate, carved mirror. I took a deep breath and tried again, "Try anything at least once," and to my huge relief, this is what came out next—

"Cry if it doesn't turn out right. Make a fool out of yourself, take a chance who knows it might work ..."

It sounded very strange and unpoetic, and I was delighted. I whooped, jumped and screamed in delight and not necessarily in that order. Both the old men were smiling from ear to ear.

"Say something," said the thin old man.

I stopped in my tracks. He was right. This was the real test. Would I rhyme?

"I should go, it's getting dark, my parents think I'm in the p ... garden."

I was cured! I had beaten the curse of Allergic Rhymitis. I reached home, and found that nobody had missed me.

"How are you feeling?" Mummy asked.

"I am feeling fine" I said. *"Can't help adding one more line,"* I muttered under my breath.

—from "A Fate Verse than Death" by Santosh Desai

1 Answer the following questions.

i What was wrong with the narrator?

ii Why had the narrator decided to run away?

iii Where did the old man in the park want to take the narrator? Why didn't the narrator like this?

iv What was Dr Ganpatadhikary's diagnosis?

v What causes alternative diseases?

____

____

____

vi What methods did Dr Ganpatadhikary try to cure the narrator?

____

____

vii Why did the narrator think that looking into a mirror would help?

____

____

viii What did the narrator discover when he reached home?

____

____

Vocabulary

1 Use the clues provided to complete the crossword. The answers are all different means of communication.

Across

1. to transmit programmes from a radio or television
5. a means of sending messages invented by Guglielmo Marconi
6. messages sent via mobile phones
7. the "world wide web"

Down

2. exchange of thoughts through spoken words
3. a letter
4. conversation between two or more people

Grammar

Clauses

Clauses are groups of words that consist of a subject and a predicate. **Main clauses** form complete thoughts and complete sentences. **Subordinate clauses** cannot stand alone as sentences and need to be attached to a main clause. **Relative clauses** modify a noun phrase and must also be attached to a main clause in order to form a complete thought.

1 Identify the underlined clauses in the sentences below.

i We were hungry because we hadn't eaten since the night before.

ii My camel, which was the tallest, brought up the rear.

iii I dropped the book that I had been reading.

iv I ate a delicious pastry and drank a cup of tea.

v Should we visit the lake, or should we stay at home?

vi That is the village where my grandfather was born.

2 Add main clauses to the following relative and subordinate clauses to make complete sentences.

i whose dog chased me around the park

____

ii because she had forgotten her keys

iii while more important events were taking place in Varanasi

iv since you have been here before

v after the engine had been repaired

vi when Harish had finished writing the letter

vii despite our obvious boredom

viii but Neha was too lazy to come with us

Writing

1 In the passage, the narrator visits a very unusual doctor. Write an account (real or fictional) of a trip to the doctor that you have taken. Were you scared or nervous?

3 The World

Comprehension

Read the passage and answer the questions.

About a three hour journey from Chennai in south India is the temple town of Tiruvannamalai. On every full moon day and especially in the month of Kartikai (November-December) it draws a pilgrim crowd of over ten lakhs. The deity is the hill itself, called Arunachala, where 'aruna' means red, bright as fire and 'achala', hill; therefore, the hill of light. The temple, built a thousand years ago, is one of the largest in India. This spot is celebrated in sacred stories, through the lives of saints who have come here and through Tamil devotional poetry for centuries. The hill has always attracted people who have reached an exalted level of spiritual understanding.

The story goes that Brahma and Vishnu once quarrelled on who was greater. Shiva manifested himself as a column of light, from which a voice issued forth that whoever could find the beginning or the end of the column would be pronounced the greater. Vishnu took the form of a boar and tunnelled deep down to find the beginning while Brahma took the form of a swan and flew up to find the end. Vishnu found that no matter how deep he went, the column was still present. He became absorbed in meditation and realised that the column had no beginning and no end and was indeed no other than his own Self. Brahma, however, grew tired of the flight and not finding the end, picked up a flower that was falling off a mountain and came back saying that he had plucked it from the top of the column! Vishnu was pronounced the greater and Brahma had to confess his deceit.

Shiva, in response to the pleas of his devotees, changed his form to a hill, and promised to manifest himself as fire, at its peak, once every year. While the figure of Nataraja expresses the dynamic form of Shiva, Arunachala expresses the stillness of being. On the full moon of Kartikai, a great fire is lit on the summit and hundreds of thousands go round the hill, a walk of about 14 kilometres.

According to an old tradition, Arunachala is said to confer moksha, or liberation from birth and death, to those who merely think of it. Ramana Maharshi, the saint whose long residence of over fifty years at Tiruvannamalai brought prominence to the town, used to emphasise the hill's spiritual vibration and its efficacy in helping the worshipper slip into an effortless state of peaceful joy.

—"The Hill at the Heart of the World" by Sharada Bhanu,
Padma Malini Raghavan and Padma Seshadri

1 Answer the following questions.

i At which time of the year does the town of Tiruvannamalai draw the greatest crowds?

ii What is the hill called? What is the meaning of this name?

iii According to the legend, what forms did Brahma and Vishnu assume?

iv In what way was Brahma deceitful? What were the consequences of his deceit?

v Why did Shiva take on the form of a hill?

vi What takes place on the full moon of Kartikai?

vii Which saint lived in Tiruvannamalai for fifty years?

Read the passage and answer the questions.

In Norse mythology, Yggdrasil is the great ash tree or the World Tree, which is the centre of the universe. This tree links and shelters all the worlds. Among the various realms that are linked to or sheltered by the tree are Asgard, or the realm of the gods, Midgard or the world of humans, Jutunheim or the land of the giants, and Helheim or the land of death.

The Voluspa, or the song of the prophets, speaks of the time when the World Tree, the wonderful Mjotvior, was just a seedling. Mjotvior means 'the wood of proper measure', symbolising a state where everything exists in a harmonious proportion. The leaves of this tree fed a goat, from whose udders flowed perpetual mead for the chief of the Norse gods, Odin's warriors, and a stag whose antlers dropped water down to Niflheim, where a well held the source of all the rivers in the nine worlds. The evergreen tree grew over two other wells of fate and wisdom.

Odin gave up one of his eyes and drank the water of the well of Mimir, that lies at the root of Yggdrasil, and acquired the wisdom to lead the Aesir, the gods, but wisdom also brought the knowledge of Ragnarok, the end, and from that day he never smiled again. He offered himself as a sacrifice to himself, for there was no greater being, and he pinned his body with his spear to Yggdrasil.

Odin hung upside down without food or drink, for nine days and nights, in a ritual that sounds strange of the warlike Vikings but would be recognised in India or in many eastern lands, as spiritual effort, tapas. Then when he was between life and death, he gained knowledge of the sacred runes or concealed wisdom, which further fitted him for his high task.

The name Yggdrasil means "terrible steed". Odin rode the tree to a destination no horse could reach. To contemplate the nine worlds upside down, implying a willingness to see from a perspective opposed to the usual one, and to connect oneself to the past, present and future is to see beyond space and time into the mystery of existence.

Yggdrasil connects not only spatially, but also temporally, to the past when the universe was in its infancy, to the present where it is the seat of assembly and sacrifice and the future when it will shake, at the time of Ragnarok.

—*"Yggdrasil the World Tree" by Sharada Bhanu, Padma Malini Raghavan and Padma Seshadri*

2 Answer the following questions.

i Which worlds does Yggdrasil shelter or link to?

____

____

ii What is the Voluspa?

iii What is the meaning of the world 'Mjotvior'?

iv How did Odin acquire wisdom to lead the gods?

v Why doesn't Odin smile?

vi How did Odin gain knowledge of the sacred runes?

vii What does the name Yggdrasil mean? Why was the tree so named?

viii What is Ragnarok?

____

____

Vocabulary

Geographical Epithets

Many cities and countries are often referred to by distinctive epithets, or descriptive terms.

1 Match the geographical epithets with place names from the box.

Ireland	Australia	Punjab	Kochi	Rome
Egypt	Chicago	Japan	Oxford	Norway

i Land of the Rising Sun ______________

ii Gift of the Nile ______________

iii Emerald Isle ______________

iv City of Seven Hills ______________

v Land of the Midnight Sun ______________

vi The Windy City ______________

vii Queen of the Arabian Sea ____________________

viii Down Under ____________________

ix City of Dreaming Spires ____________________

x The Land of Five Rivers ____________________

Grammar

Brackets

Brackets, or parentheses, contain additional information that could be left out without making the sentence meaningless. Without this information the sentence would still make sense (and would still be a complete sentence), but the information in parentheses adds meaning to the sentence.

For example:

My coat (which is made of wool) was wet and uncomfortable.

The dog (who is afraid of loud noises) spends Diwali hiding under the table.

1 Rewrite the following sentences using brackets.

i In England where I lived for many years football is more popular than cricket.

____

____

ii If you are tired and everyone is tired on the third day you may rest in the evening.

____

____

iii The food which was an unappetising shade of grey was as tasteless as it looked.

____

____

iv My mother who studied medicine and my father who is a mathematician have been married for twenty years.

____

____

v This car runs on electricity rather than petrol or diesel but this does not mean it does not rely on fossil fuels.

____

____

vi Although it is possible to extract DNA from hair and also blood, epithelial cells and bone marrow, this cannot yet be used for purposes beyond identification.

____

vii Dr Swaminathan Alisha's mother will be giving a talk on the life cycle of lobsters.

viii Aswath a charming young man of my acquaintance collects the books of Richmal Crompton.

ix Souvlaki a Greek preparation of grilled meat or vegetables was Ashok's favourite dish, but he would eat practically anything.

x Read chapter six pages 304-327 for more information on volcanoes.

Writing

1 Read the conversation between a group of people and rewrite it in reported speech.

"I suppose we're all going in for this same exam!" said Winona. It broke the ice. Everybody looked relieved. The atmosphere seemed to clear.

"Yes, we're all going in—that's right enough," replied a tall girl in spectacles, "but there are only two scholarships, so nineteen of us are bound to fail."

"Whew! A nice cheering prospect. Wish they'd put us out of our misery at once!" groaned a girl with a long fair pigtail.

"I'm all upset!" shivered another.

"It's like a game of musical chairs," suggested a fourth. "We're all scrambling for the same thing, and some are bound to be out of it."

The tall girl laughed nervously.

"Suppose we've got to take our sporting luck!" she murmured.

"If nineteen are sure to lose, two are sure to win at any rate," said Winona. "That's logic and mathematics and all the rest of it, too!"

"Right you are! That's a more cheering creed! It doesn't do to cry too soon!" chirped a jolly-looking dark-eyed girl with a red hair ribbon. "'Never say die till you're dead' is my motto!"

"I'm wearing a mascot," said a short, pale girl, exhibiting her charm, which hung from a chain round her neck. "I never am lucky, so I thought I'd try what this would do for me for once. I know English history beautifully down to the end of Queen Anne, and no further, and if they set any questions on the Georges I'll be stumped."

"I've learnt Africa, but Asia would floor me!" observed another, looking up from a geography book, in which she was making a last desperate clutch at likely items of knowledge. "I never can remember which side of India Madras is on; I get it mixed up with Bombay."

"I wish to goodness they'd go ahead and begin," mourned the owner of the red hair ribbon. "It's this waiting that knocks the spirit out of me. Patience isn't my pet virtue. I call it cruelty to animals to leave us on tenterhooks."

4 Art and Culture

Comprehension

Read the passage and answer the questions.

The haiku has deceptively simple rules: poetry in seventeen syllables. Matsuo Basho travelled all over his country, breaking down his life and the world into just that: seventeen syllables.

He published his first haiku in 1662, when he was eighteen years old. By 1684, at forty, he had become famous, the simplicity of his writing style bringing out intense feelings and vivid observations of nature and life. But he felt a little lonely, so he set out.

He had no particular destination in mind when he began from the city now known as Tokyo. He ended up going to Mount Fuji, the city of

Kyoto, the region of Ueno and other areas in southern Honshu Island.

He had a reason for not having a plan: the Japanese countryside was then full of murderous robbers and outlaws. Few travelled the way he did, unarmed and on foot, accompanied here and there by wandering monks or apprentice poets who wanted to learn from him.

He was back home a year later, in 1685, where he met his friends and shared the haikus he had written during his travels. Reflecting on what he had seen, he wrote some more poems, including a very famous one about a frog.

Three years after his return, he was off on another road trip to the countryside. Along the way, his poems became barer and barer, stripped of fancy words and phrases, just a collection of words with so many different layers of meaning to them that people are still studying and interpreting them today. This road trip lasted a year. On his return, he had barely settled in at home when he decided to journey north. Over a little less than six months, Basho travelled 2,400 km on foot, going to the farthest northern parts of the main island of Japan. In 1691, he returned home.

In 1694, he left his hut once again for, as he told his disciples, one more journey. This time he went to Kyoto and Osaka. But his frugal, almost mendicant-like life, hard travelling and bad weather had made him weak and he died—as he might have wanted to—on the road in Osaka.

His friends collected his poems and published them and we can still read them today: some of the greatest lines on human life and the world in which we make our individual journeys.

—*"The Travel-Worn Satchel" by Siddhartha Sarma*

1 Answer the following questions.

i Which country did Matsuo Basho come from?

____

ii What made Matsuo Basho famous?

iii Why didn't Basho have a plan when he left Tokyo?

iv Who were his fellow-travellers?

v How did his poetry change while he was travelling?

vi How far did Basho travel?

vii Where and why did Basho die?

____

____

Read the passage and answer the questions.

There have been many artists whose travels influenced their paintings. Only a few travelled to so far and different a place from their native shores that they came up with wholly new interpretations of their art. Fewer still changed the evolution of art itself. Paul Gauguin travelled to the other end of the world and found ...

Actually, he found himself in a different land very early in his life: when he was three, in 1851, his parents left France for Peru. This land and its culture would influence his paintings later. Returning to France, he joined the Navy, becoming a stockbroker afterwards.

By 1887, he had taken to painting full time and travelled to Panama, which then was much different from the canal country we know today. In its wilds, he found colour, meaning and form which entered through different stages into his paintings.

That was the Impressionist period in painting, but Gauguin could not connect to it, being more drawn to the artistic styles of Africa and Asia. By 1891, he had had enough of European culture and art and sailed off—to the Pacific. Here, on the tiny island (well, all the islands in those parts are tiny) of Tahiti, Gauguin set up camp in a village. He looked back on what he had seen in South and Central America and the Pacific islands and began to paint.

First, he came up with paintings on general life in Tahiti. These started a new trend in art, called primitivism, in which the simple existence is held up as an example to follow. Then he painted his masterpiece: *Where Do We Come From? What Are We? Where Are We*

Going? Over a vast canvas, he spelt out his vision of human life from its origin to final destiny. Though the art was heavily influenced by his life in Tahiti, anyone who sees it today (it's in a museum in Boston) will understand what Gauguin was trying to say.

He painted much more in this, the most creative phase of his life. These paintings would influence later artists to develop newer forms of expression.

So today when we see a Gauguin, we know that one of the greatest painters who ever lived found his best method of expression after crossing to the other end of the world.

—*"Return to the Pastoral" by Siddhartha Sarma*

2 Answer the following questions.

i To which country did Gauguin travel as a child?

____

____

ii What style of painting was popular in Europe at the time?

____

____

iii To where did Gauguin travel in 1887?

____

____

iv Where did he travel in 1891?

v Which styles of art appealed to Gauguin?

vi Where did Gauguin settle down?

vii Which new trend in art did Gauguin start? Describe it.

viii Where is Gauguin's art today?

Vocabulary

1 Match the following idioms with their meanings.

i	to face the music	a	to completely change one's opinion
ii	fit as a fiddle	b	to do things differently from everyone else
iii	to change one's tune	c	to occupy a less important position than someone else
iv	music to one's ears	d	to be sold for a very low price
v	to make a song and dance about something	e	to take events as they come, rather than having a definite plan
vi	to blow your own trumpet	f	to draw attention to something
vii	to go for a song	g	to be very healthy
viii	to play second fiddle	h	to accept the consequences
ix	to play it by ear	i	to boast of one's own achievements
x	to march to the beat of a different drum	j	exactly what one wants to hear

Grammar

Modals

Modal verbs are a type of auxiliary (helping) verbs. They cannot be used as a main verb in a sentence. They deal with the concepts of necessity and possibility. Some common modal verbs are can, could, ought to, shall, may, might, must, should, will, would.

1 Fill in the blanks with an appropriate modal verb.

i Aishwarya ________________ have finished writing the book by now.

ii Shruti ________________ speak three languages.

iii She ________________ have studied abroad, but chose not to.

iv Amit and Abey ________________ be fighting again.

v Rohit ________________ come to Delhi next month.

vi Before you go I ________________ show you our garden.

vii Avni ________________ be here by now.

viii If you are planning to stay in the desert all night you

________________ carry mosquito repellent.

Writing

1 **Write a review of a movie that you have recently watched. Remember to give the reader such details as the title of the movie, the name of the director and the names of the main actors. Also remember not to give away the ending!**

5 War and Peace

Comprehension

Read the passage and answer the questions.

Alchemists had two important goals that kept them motivated. Their first goal was to find a way to convert common metals into gold or silver. And their second goal was to create the elixir of life. Ironically, it is this second goal that led them to invent gunpowder, which is hardly conducive to life.

The invention of gunpowder changed the course of human history. Once it was introduced to the battlefield, all the rules of war began to change. Now one did not have to rely on the power of human muscles to operate a weapon. Gunpowder made it possible to shoot projectiles further and faster than ever before. Guns are so common nowadays that it is hard to imagine a world without them. Let us look at some of the weapons that existed before gunpowder was invented.

Bows and arrows have existed since prehistoric times. A skilled archer could shoot an arrow with great accuracy. If you wanted to hurl something nasty at your enemy, you could use a trebuchet (an engine of war for hurling stones). The largest trebuchet could throw objects as big as a cow several hundred feet across with reasonable accuracy. People have used the trebuchet to hurl rocks, beehives, barrels of boiling hot oil and even heads of captured prisoners at their enemies!

A battering ram was another weapon that was commonly used. In those days, there was usually one massive door that kept an entire fort protected. A large group of soldiers would use all their strength to drive a huge ram through this door.

Boiling oil was also used as a weapon. Castles were built with special openings through which people could pour boiling oil, hot pitch or heated sand on their enemies who were trying to enter their castles.

Although the alchemists failed to get what they were looking for, they discovered that an explosive mixture could be produced by mixing sulphur, charcoal and saltpetre (potassium nitrate). This mixture finally led to the invention of gunpowder.

Gunpowder was invented in China. The exact date of invention remains unknown. Gunpowder was first used in AD 904 in a war against the Mongols. The Chinese used gunpowder to build an inflammable projectile called "flying fire", a tube of gunpowder attached to an arrow. When you lit it, the arrow would propel itself exactly like a rocket and strike the enemy.

People believe that the idea of gunpowder spread to other civilisations through the silk route. (This was one of the most famous historical trade routes of the world.) Gunpowder was important to the Chinese. The projectiles and rockets invented by them gave them an edge in warfare. It was also psychologically overwhelming for the enemy because they had never seen anything like that before and it left them completely devastated.

By the thirteenth century, explosive projectiles were being used by the Mongols in their invasions of Japan. The Arabs acquired the knowledge of gunpowder sometime between AD 1240 and AD 1280. The first cannon in history is believed to have been fired by the Mamluks against the Mongols at the battle of Ain Jalut in AD 1260.

The knowledge of gunpowder reached Europe in the thirteenth century. Around the late fourteenth century, European powder-makers began to add liquid to reduce the dust. With the dust gone, the risk of explosion was greatly reduced.

Then they shaped the resulting paste of moist gunpowder into granules and left them to dry. Gunmen found that these granules were much more powerful and easier to load into guns. The same granulation process is used today in the pharmaceutical industry to make tablets. This ensures that each tablet contains the same proportion of the actual medicine.

What are some of the effects gunpowder has had on society? After gunpowder was invented, people had to rebuild their forts. During the medieval period, castles had high walls to keep out attackers. But now their forts had to withstand artillery bombardments. To do this, engineers designed a special kind of fortress. These fortresses had low, thick, sloping walls that would either absorb or glance off cannon fire. They were also shaped like stars with bastions protruding at sharp angles. This made sure that every bastion could be supported with fire from an adjacent bastion.

Another effect that gunpowder had on society was that the aristocracy lost the power that they had once enjoyed. Their 200 to 400 year-old castles could no longer defend them against their enemies. Also, the cavalry, which was made up of the elite, lost much of its importance.

—*from* Why We Are Where We Are: A Brief History of the Universe *by Swagata Deb and Supriya Seshadri*

1 **Answer the following questions.**

i Who do you think were the alchemists? What were their goals?

____

____

ii In what ways did the introduction of gunpowder change the rules of war?

____

____

iii What were trebuchets?

____

____

iv Where and when was gunpowder first used?

____

____

v What was 'flying fire'?

____

____

vi How did the knowledge of gunpowder spread to the rest of the world?

vii When was the first cannon used?

viii What change did European powder-makers bring about? How was this helpful?

ix In what ways did the structures of fortresses change after the invention of gunpowder?

Vocabulary

1 Match the following idioms with the word "throw" in them to their meanings.

i	throw the book at someone	a	show willingness to enter a (usually political) competition
ii	throw down the gauntlet	b	throw away useful things in the process of getting rid of useless things
iii	throw in the towel	c	punish someone to the fullest extent of the law
iv	throw one's hat into the ring	d	spoil someone's plans
v	throw a spanner into the works	e	issue a challenge to someone
vi	throw the baby out with the bathwater	f	express a desire to quit

Grammar

Gerunds

Gerunds end in the letters **ing** and look like verbs. However, they function as nouns within a sentence.

1 In which of the following sentences are the underlined words gerunds?

i A little learning is a dangerous thing.

ii We were sitting in the garden when we saw the shooting star.

iii Bharti is wrapping the present because Sukanya is busy.

iv Akbar's quick thinking saved the day.

v Unfortunately, we had to sample Shashi's terrible cooking.

vi Tomorrow I will be travelling to Jaisalmer.

vii Bull-fighting is a popular tourist attraction in Spain.

viii The men are loading the truck with cabbages.

Writing

1 The paragraph contains a number of frequently misspelled words. Can you spot the errors? Rewrite the passage, removing all the spelling mistakes.

The playwrites spent alot of time arguing over where they should preform the play. Some times it seemed as if arguing was their favourite passtime. Kiran argued that the small theatre simply could not accomodate the audience, but Hartosh beleived that in a larger space the wierd sound effects that were so vital to the play would dissapear, and the actors would be invisable against the black backdrop. Changable as always, Kailash began by agreeing with Kiran, but ended up siding with Hartosh. The descision had to be made quickly because both venues' calenders were rappidly filling up. There were other problems as well; the actors' names had been mispelt on the programme, and the fake marble colum that they were using as a stage prop had broken. After the sucess of the preceeding year they could not let the company down.

6 Mysteries

Comprehension

Read the poem and answer the questions.

There was a man in our town,
Half beggar, half rapscallion,
Who, just because his eyes were brown,
Was thought to be Italian:
And, though with much insistence
He said that people erred,
And bitterly to Italy
He frequently referred,
The false report, as is the way

Of false reports, had come to stay!

So every one who'd been to Rome
By aid of Cook's or Gaze's,
Would call upon him at home
To flaunt Italian phrases.
"Capite Questa lingua?"
The inquiry would be:
"Pochissimo? Benissimo!
Vi prego, ditemi,
Siete voi contento qua,
Lontano dall' Italia?"

The victim, plunged in deep disgust,
Grew nervous, could not slumber;
Said he, "I'm called Italian, just
Because my eyes are umber,
And if this persecution
Is ever to be stopped,
Some stern and stoic, hard, heroic
Course I must adopt!"
And so, to everyone's surprise,
He calmly scratched out both his eyes!

The neighbours said: "So strange a thing
Might seem to be an omen.
We thought his wits were wandering,
But now we know they're Roman!"
And so at him by legions,
By bevies, hosts, and herds,
Professors, purists, tramps, and tourists
Screamed Italian words.
Perceiving all he'd done was vain,
He scratched his eyesight in again.

The moral: If your neighbors say
    You're one thing or another,
You'll find there isn't any way
    Their prejudice to smother.
What matter if they think you
    From Italy or Greece?
I beg you, treasure no displeasure:
    Bow and hold your peace.
        Like Omar, underneath the bow
        You'll find there's paradise enow!

—*"The Mysterious Misapprehension Concerning a Man in our Town"*
by Guy Wetmore Carryl

1 Answer the following questions.

i Why was the man thought to be Italian?

____

____

ii "The false report, as is the way/ Of false reports, had come to stay!" Explain these lines.

____

____

iii Why did people visit the man at home?

____

____

iv What drastic action did the man take? What was the reasoning behind it?

v Did the man's solution work?

vi What is the moral provided by the poet? Do you agree with it?

vii "He scratched his eyesight in again". Comment.

viii Do you think this is a funny or a serious poem? Give reasons for your answer.

Vocabulary

1 **Using a dictionary, find the meanings of the following words from the poem. Then use the words in sentences of your own.**

i rapscallion

____

ii stoic

____

iii umber

____

iv prejudice

____

v flaunt

____

vi persecution

____

vii smother

____

viii bevy

____

ix misapprehension

____

Antonyms

> Antonyms are pairs of words with opposite meanings.

2 Find antonyms for the following words in the poem.

i lenient ________________

ii pragmatic ________________

iii cowardly ________________

iv relaxed ________________

v soared ________________

vi protection ________________

vii tolerance ________________

viii murmured ________________

Grammar

Infinitives

The infinitive is the basic form of a verb, usually preceded by "to".

For example:

to eat, to play, to run

Infinitives can be used as nouns, adjectives or adverbs.

When it occurs after some verbs (such as feel, hear, make, see, let, help) the infinitive is not preceded by "to".

1 Underline the infinitives in the following sentences. Can you identify the part of speech in each case?

i The family went out to celebrate the good news.

____

ii All she wanted was to sleep comfortably for one night.

____

iii We brought Shilpa some movies to watch while she was ill.

____

iv To err is human, to forgive, divine.

____

v Shivam ran after Ishaan to thank him for all his help.

____

vi We will have to wait until after the class.

____

2 **Choose whether the gerund or the infinitive is correct.**

i Mahima offered (to help/helping) Pranav with his homework.

ii Samuel is too busy (to come/coming) with us.

iii The club prohibits (to swim/swimming) during the winter months.

iv Rajam would like (to know/knowing) where you bought those gloves.

v Vasundhara and Chirag both take (to drive/driving) lessons.

vi The others left but Annie decided (to stay/staying).

vii We all disliked (to drink/drinking) our milk.

viii Luckily this time I remembered (to pack/packing) my toothbrush.

3 **Rewrite the following sentences, replacing the gerunds with infinitives and the infinitives with gerunds.**

i The students liked to pluck ripe mulberries from the trees near the playground.

____

____

ii Try cleaning this house before the guests arrive.

____

____

iii After each party they would start singing and continue until it was time to go home.

iv We began to whisper to each other as soon as the teacher left the room.

v My brother continues to work at the factory even though he hates it.

vi Kriti loves drawing the small birds and animals that she finds in her garden.

vii Sister Augusta loved playing table tennis and could beat the school champion at the game.

viii The class continued to shout despite the protests of the new teacher.

ix Jaspreet prefers sleeping on a feather bed.

x Everyone always seems to start laughing whenever I say anything.

Writing

1 Write an informal letter to a friend in another city. Describe the recent events that have taken place in your own city.

7 The Future

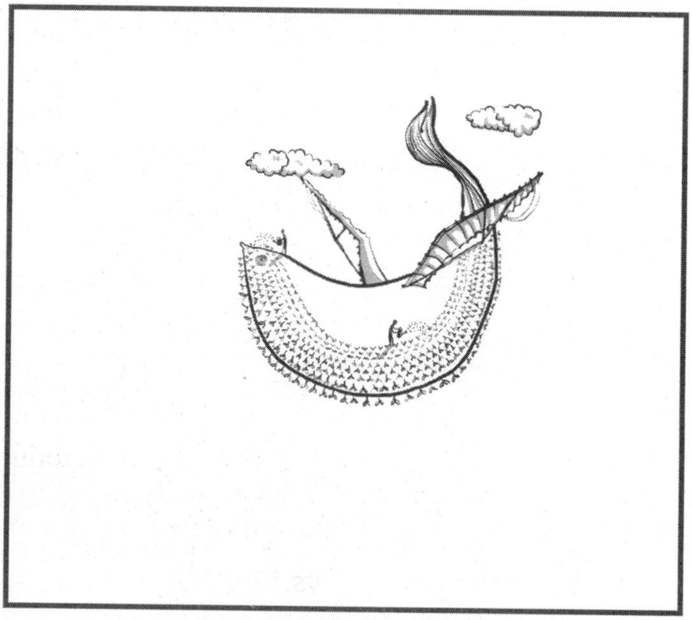

Comprehension

Read the passage and answer the questions.

Is there a possibility that life exists on other planets? We haven't found any evidence of life on the other planets of our solar system. But that doesn't mean anything. There is an enormous amount of space in the universe. There doesn't seem to be anything special about our galaxy or our sun for that matter.

Of course, there is a difference between life and intelligent life. Scientists disagree about the possibility of intelligence evolving on another planet. Some of them believe that it takes very special conditions for intelligence to evolve. Others argue that the evolutionary process encourages the growth of intelligence.

If an alien did visit us, what would he look like? He would probably have two eyes. Everything on earth that lives in light has developed eyes. Having two eyes would give the alien a sense of depth and increase his chances of catching his prey. The alien would have more than one limb if he is building spaceships and so on. But the number would be definitely less than twenty, because it would take an enormous amount of brain power to co-ordinate all of them.

The distance between stars is so great that scientists don't expect them to visit us. But some of them believe that there is a strong possibility that aliens do exist.

Can we colonise space?

How long do you think the human race will survive? A collapsing universe would certainly put an end to all life. But that may not happen for a hundred billion years. Before that, our sun will become a red giant and engulf the entire solar system. But that won't happen for several billion years either. What we should be worried about is that mankind has the capability to bring about its own extinction in less than a decade!

This can be achieved in several ways. With genetic manipulation, scientists can create new forms of life. What if someone produced a deadly strain of virus against which there was no protection? Less than a thousandth ounce of a certain bacterial toxin is enough to wipe out the entire human population. Then there is 'global warming'. Our air now contains fifteen per cent more carbon dioxide than it did hundred years ago. If it increases at its present rate, there will be a climatic catastrophe in the twenty-first century.

Nuclear power plants are also a cause of concern. A tiny leak may cause millions of deaths. Nuclear waste may also be fatal to all human life.

We perform highly dangerous experiments on earth. For example, with the help of lasers, recent techniques have produced conditions that are found only at the centre of the sun. How can we be sure of the safety of such experiments?

For these reasons, many people in the scientific community think that we should consider the colonisation of space. But what exactly is space colonisation? It is the concept of self-sufficient human habitation at various locations in space.

Earth's atmosphere contains exactly the right amount of oxygen, water vapour and other gases for us to breathe; is thick enough to protect us from harmful radiation and thin enough so that we don't get crushed by its weight. How could we achieve these conditions on another planet?

We can go about it in three different ways. We could create a habitat which would support life, but be completely isolated from the environment. Or, we could modify the environment of a planet to suit our needs. This is known as "terra-forming". Most people have Mars in mind, when they are talking about terra-formation. Theoretically it is possible to deliberately alter the environment of another planet. However, the money required for this process is far beyond what anyone is willing to spend, and we do not know how long it would take or what practical difficulties might arise.

The third option is even more drastic. We could use genetic engineering to change organisms to become compatible with the new environment. Science fiction uses the terms "cyborgs" and "transhumans" to refer to such creatures and people who are in favour of this procedure are known as transhumanists.

Although many scientists believe that colonisation of space is necessary, others are violently opposed to the idea. They think that instead of spending so much money on space research, we should be using it to feed the poor in the world. They argue that space colonisation would be a huge project and that we just don't have the technology that is needed to carry it out.

We don't know whether space colonisation will be possible in the near future or not, but let me tell you what Larry Niven, a well-known science fiction author had to say about this: "The dinosaurs became extinct because they didn't have a space programme. And if we become extinct because we don't have a space programme, it'll serve us right!"

—*from* Why We Are Where We Are: A Brief History of the Universe *by Swagata Deb and Supriya Seshadri*

1 Answer the following questions.

i Why do scientists disagree about the possibility of intelligent life developing on other planets?

____

____

ii What might a creature from another planet look like? Why?

____

____

iii In what ways might humankind bring about its own destruction?

____

____

iv Why do many people think that humankind should attempt to colonise space?

____

____

v What is 'terra-forming'?

____

____

vi Why hasn't terra-formation been attempted?

____

____

vii Who are transhumanists?

____

____

viii Why do some scientists argue against space colonisation? Do you agree with them?

____

____

Vocabulary

Retronyms

What do the following words or phrases have in common?

(a) landline

(b) black-and-white television

(c) acoustic guitar

All these words are retronyms.

A retronym is a phrase that is coined to describe the older version of something after a new version has been invented.

For example: people only began to use the phrase "black-and-white television" after colour televisions became popular.

1 Circle the phrases that are retronyms. What developments or inventions caused these phrases to be coined?

snail mail	flat-screen tv	fake fur
mobile phone	field hockey	silent film
World War I	analogue watch	gel pen
hardcover book	soft copy	classical music

Grammar

Split Infinitives

A split infinitive occurs when another word (or words) is placed between to and the infinitive form of a verb.

For example:

Little Red Riding Hood was warned to never walk alone in the woods.

The bell rang and we began to quickly gather our belongings.

1 Rewrite the following sentences by removing the split infinitive in each case.

i The government plans to gradually phase out the old buses.

____

____

ii Salman needs to really work hard if he wants to enter the tournament.

____

____

iii Many grammarians tell us to not split infinitives.

____

____

iv Vinay will have to take extra coaching in order to not fail the course.

____

____

v My grandmother ordered me to never divulge her secret recipe for ginger chicken.

vi I used to secretly admire her for her courage.

vii My sister used to always demand an ice cream when we went to the beach.

viii Tulika and Neha seem to constantly bunk class in order to play basketball.

ix You were clearly instructed to not open the envelope until the bell had rung.

x Upon discovering that the tourists had no money, the children began to aggressively shout at them.

Writing

1 **What do you think the world will be like a century from now? Write a short story about a character from the present who travels into the future.**

Acknowledgements

The publishers would like to thank the following authors, illustrators and publishers for permission to use their materials:

Garima Gupta for the theme page illustrations; Santosh Desai for "A Fate Verse Than Death" from *City Stories* (Scholastic India: 2008); Sharada Bhanu, Padma Malini Raghavan and Padma Seshadri for "The Hill at the Heart of the World" and "Yggdrasil, the World Tree" from *103 Myths, Legends, Fables and Stuff* (Scholastic India: 2008); Siddhartha Sarma for "The Travel-Worn Satchel" and "Return to the Pastoral" from *103 Journeys, Trips, Voyages and Stuff* (Scholastic India: 2007); Swagata Deb and Supriya Seshadri for "How We Learned to Blow Up Things – The Invention of Gunpowder" and "Are We Alone in the Universe?" from *Why We Are Where We Are: A Brief History of the Universe* (Scholastic India: 2009).

While every attempt has been made to trace copyright holders for the text and illustrations, this has not been possible in all cases. Any omissions brought to our attention will be rectified in future editions.